A Magic Mouse Guide

Computers

by

Chris Ward-Johnson
and the Magic Mouse

Illustrations & layout by
Laughing Gravy Design

CHERRYTREE BOOKS

Editor's note
Computers and software vary considerably. In this book we present information that is generally true of all personal computers and show a variety of particular screens. Do not worry if your screen is not the same as the one that appears in the book.

Acknowledgments
The publishers would like to thank the following for permission to use their photographs and copyright material:
Apple Computer; Eudora; Microsoft; Netscape UK Ltd.

Also thanks to: Steve Gridley (photography), David Osbaldestin.

A CHERRYTREE BOOK

Designed and produced by A S Publishing.

Illustrations and layout by Gary Dillon & Phil Jolly
at Laughing Gravy Design Limited.

First published 1999 by Cherrytree Press Ltd
327 High St
Slough
Berkshire SL1 1TX

In memory of Jonathan Inglis

British Library Cataloguing in Publication Data
Ward-Johnson, Chris
Computers. - (Magic Mouse Guides)
1. Microcomputers - Juvenile Literature
I. Title
004.1'6
ISBN 1-84234-078-6

Printed and bound in Belgium by Proost International Book Production.

Contents

Mouse tips

Don't worry if your screen does not always look exactly like the ones in the book.

Mouse tips

If there are words you don't understand, look on pages 28-31.

A personal computer

Today is Ben's birthday. His present is in a big box. Inside are lots more boxes and bags and packing material.

"Hooray," shouts Ben. "It's a PC – my own computer. Thanks Mum. Thanks Dad."

Ben's sister Liza helps him to set up the computer. She plugs in leads that join the parts together. Then she plugs it all in to the electricity.

The computer's parts

Ben's computer has a monitor that looks like a television screen. It has a keyboard, a mouse and a printer.

The most important part is the box that holds the computer's brain. This is made up of the CPU, the hard disk drive and the memory.

The CPU does the work. The hard disk drive contains instructions that tell the CPU what work to do and how to do it. The memory stores information.

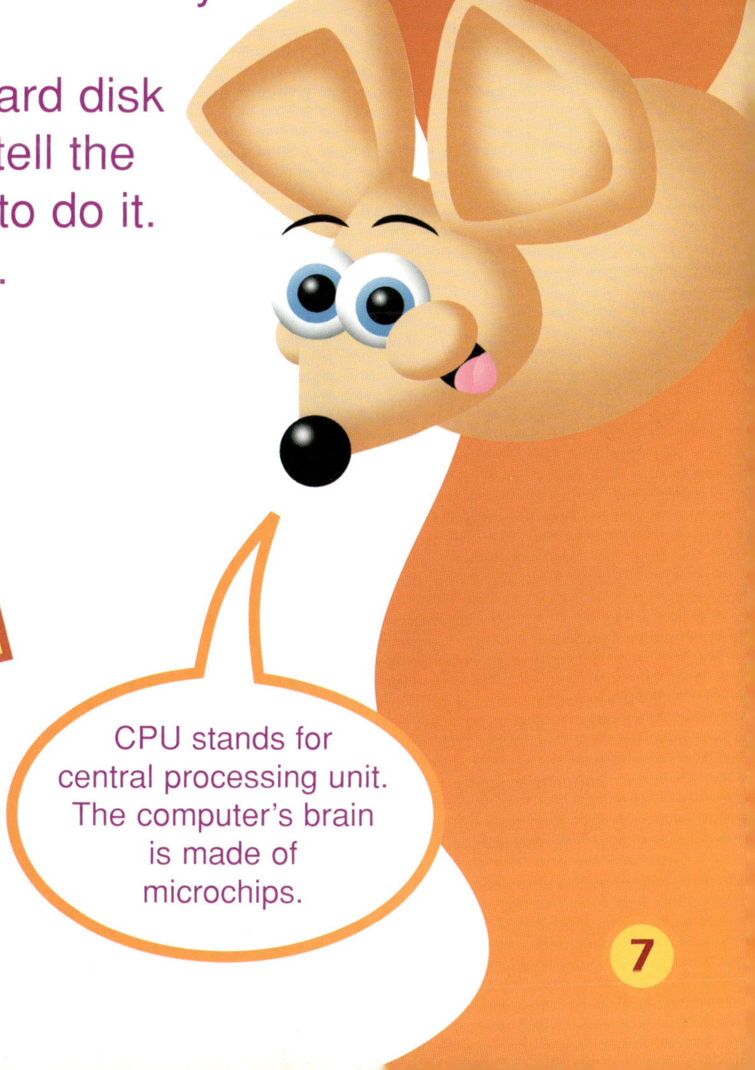

The keyboard

When all the parts are linked up, Ben presses the button and waits for his computer to start. Soon it goes ‘ping’ and the screen lights up.

Ben can’t wait to start. He taps at the keyboard. There are keys on it for each letter of the alphabet. There are keys for the numbers 1 to 9 and 0.

There is a key that lets you write in CAPITAL LETTERS and loads more that help you use the computer.

The letters you type on the keyboard appear on the screen.

Press the shift key to make capital letters. Look in the manual to see what the other keys do.

The mouse

You use the mouse for pointing at things on the screen. The mouse moves a cursor. This can be an arrow, a little line or some other symbol. It shows you where you are on the screen.

The mouse rests on a mouse mat to protect it from the desk. As you move the mouse on the mat, the cursor moves on the screen. You click the mouse to make something happen. An hour glass or a watch tell you to wait a moment.

Ben tries to move the cursor with the mouse. It goes all over the place.

Practise using your mouse. It soon gets easier. Remember to look after your mouse. Keep it clean. Use your mouse only on the mat.

Hard copy and Help

The monitor displays on the screen the words and figures you type on the keyboard. It also displays pictures that the computer produces.

You can use the printer to print out the work you do on the screen. When you print your work on paper, it is called hard copy.

It takes time to learn how to use a PC. Practise as much as you can. Don't worry if you get things wrong at first. If you have problems, look in the manual or click on Help.

Hardware and software

Ben practises on the keyboard. He learns how to control the mouse. Now he wants to write a letter.

"Now's the time to use your birthday present from me," says Liza. Liza's present was a software program.

All the bits of a computer you can see are called hardware. A software program is a set of instructions. It tells the hardware what to do. It is like a driver controlling a car. A computer needs software to make it do useful work.

Software comes on disks. They may be floppy disks,compact disks or DVDs. Compact disks are called CDs like music disks.

Liza shows Ben how to load the disk on to his computer. She is careful not to touch the shiny side.

The operating system

Every computer comes with one set of programs already on its hard disk. The most important program is the operating system.

A computer cannot run other programs without an operating system. When you switch on the computer, the operating system springs into action. It tells the computer what gadgets are linked to it. It tells it what programs have been loaded.

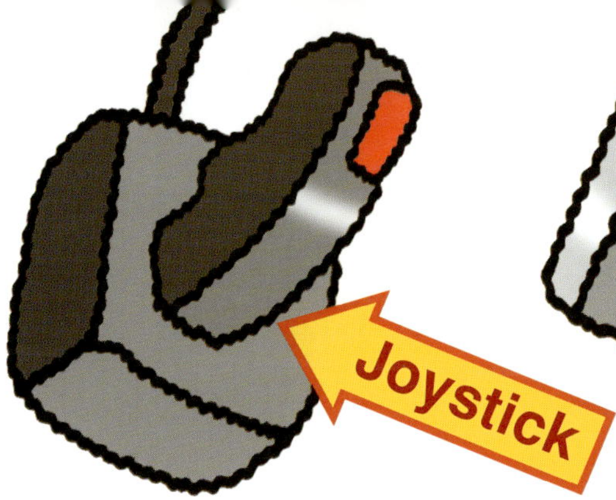

You can attach all sorts of gadgets to computers:

- Printers
- Joysticks for playing games.
- Scanners for copying pictures.
- Digital cameras for seeing your photos on screen.
- Modems that let you send e-mails and faxes.
- Computer pens for drawing on the screen.
- Music keyboards for playing and writing music.

Word processing

Ben's new software program is a word processor. A word processor lets you type anything you like. You can correct mistakes. You can move words and sentences about. You can also check your spelling.

A word processor can help you make your work look smart. You can use big letters or small ones and different kinds of type. You can lay out your work in all sorts of ways.

BIG TYPE

small TYPE

Always read through your work. Your spell checker will not tell you if you have written rat instead of cat.

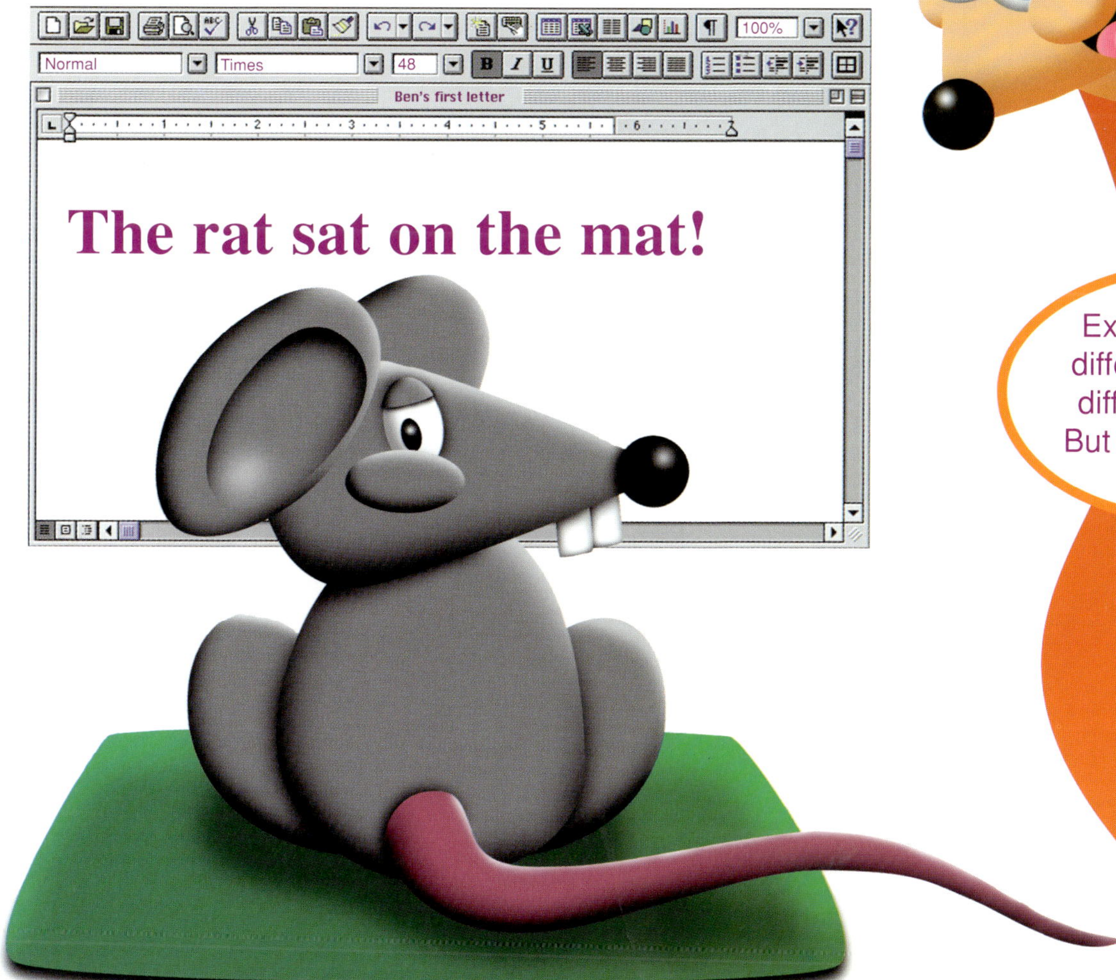

Experiment with different type and different layouts. But keep it simple.

Icons and menus

When you load a software program on to your computer a little picture appears. The picture is called an icon.

Ben uses his mouse to point at the icon. He clicks the mouse to start up the program. Now more words and icons appear at the top of the screen. Ben clicks on the first one. A menu of choices drops down. Ben selects one that lets him start a document. This is a blank page with a window round it.

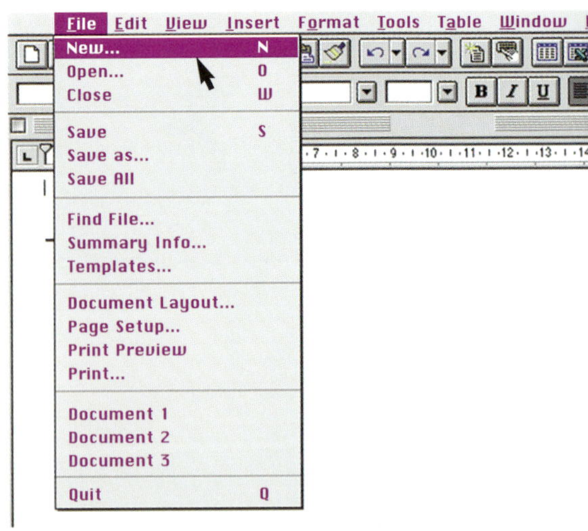

Ben types his letter in the window.
"That looks great," says Liza.
"Let's print it."

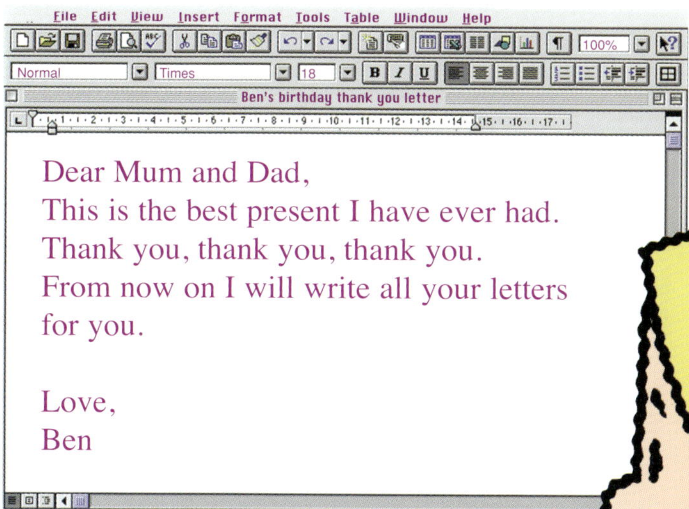

Ben's birthday thank you letter

Dear Mum and Dad,
This is the best present I have ever had.
Thank you, thank you, thank you.
From now on I will write all your letters for you.

Love,
Ben

Windows and dialog boxes

Ben clicks on an icon that looks like a printer. A window full of words appears on the screen. It is a dialog box. It asks Ben how many copies he wants. It asks lots of other questions.

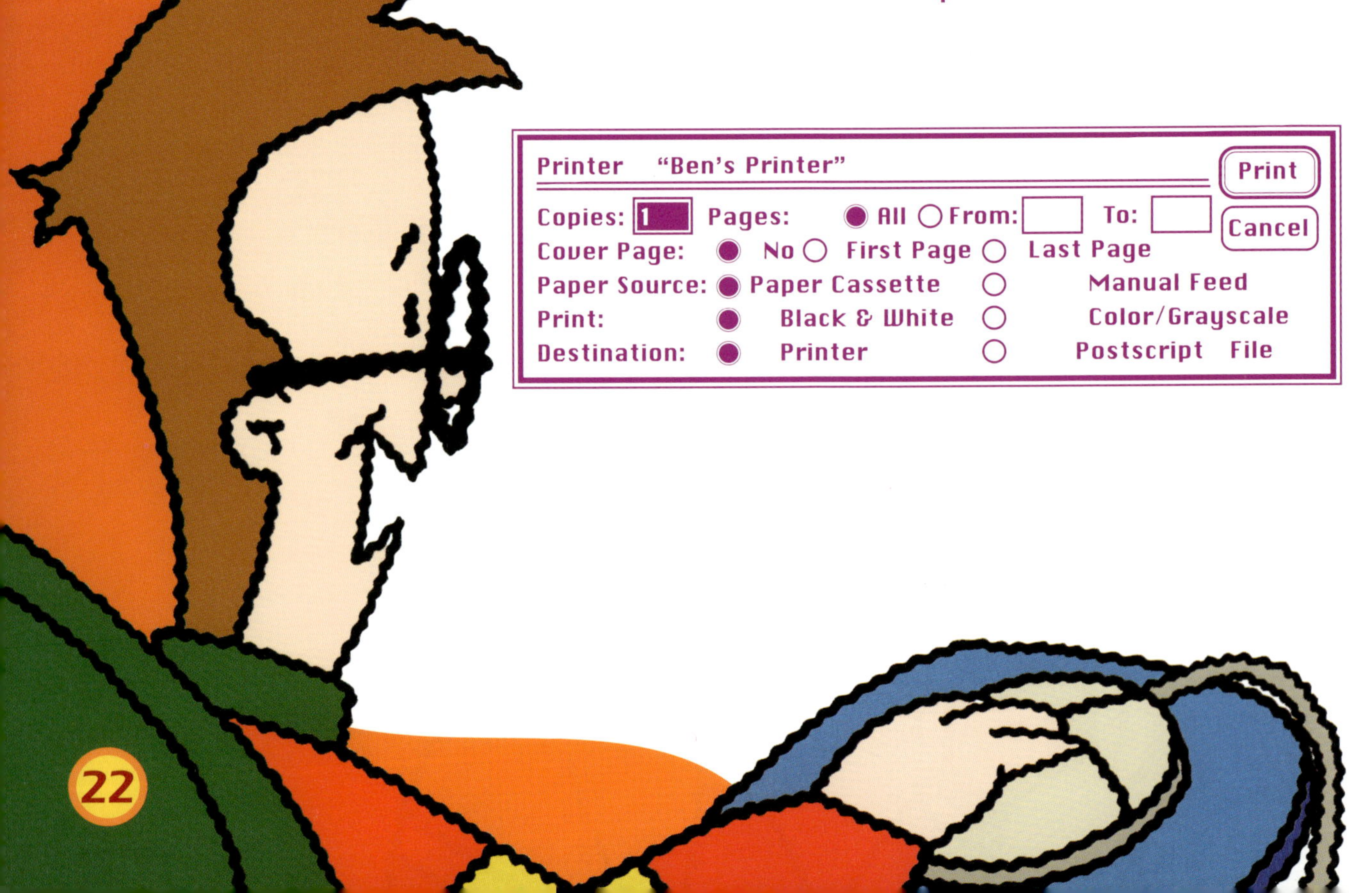

Ben clicks his answers and clicks the Print button. In a few seconds his letter comes out of the printer.

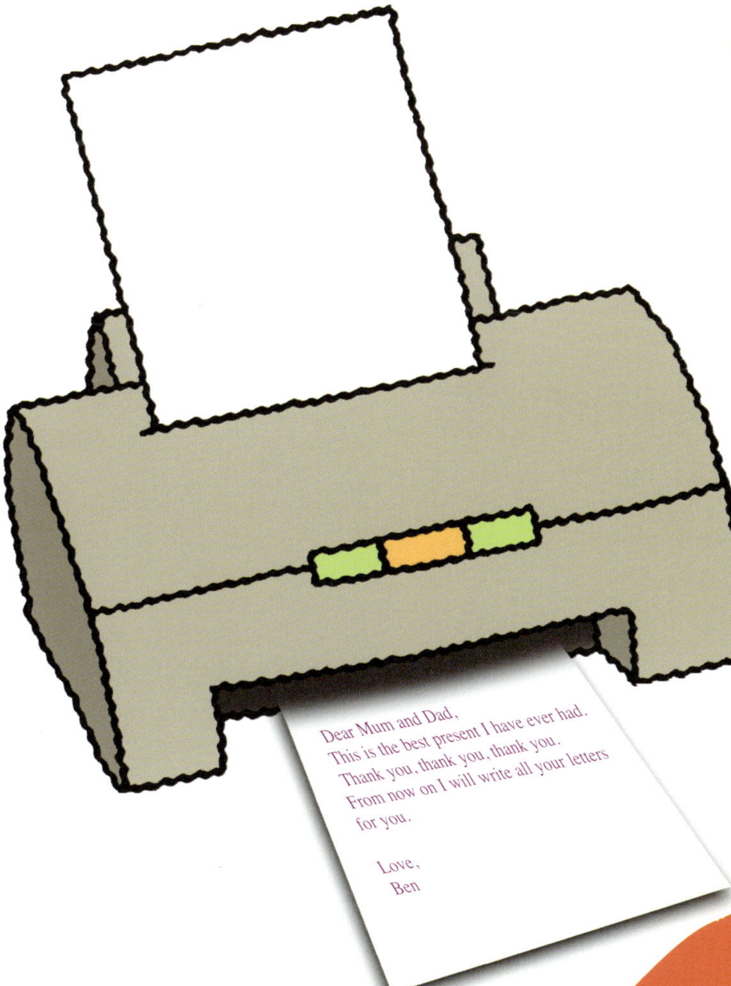

Pictures and games

Next Ben wants to draw a picture on his PC. But he cannot because he does not have a paint program. Liza has one. She can draw lines with the mouse and use computer paintbrushes to colour her pictures.

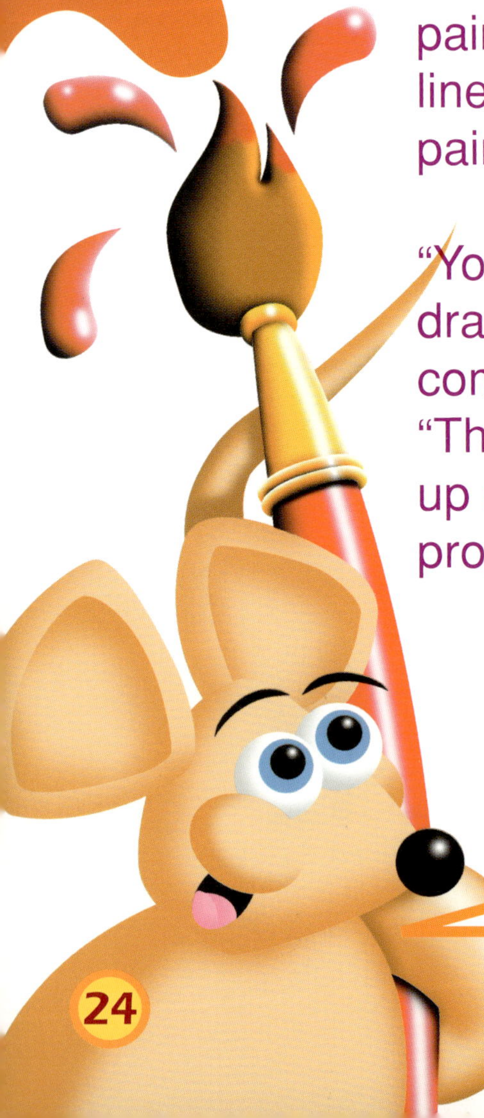

"You can practise drawing on my computer," says Liza. "Then you can save up and buy a paint program for yourself."

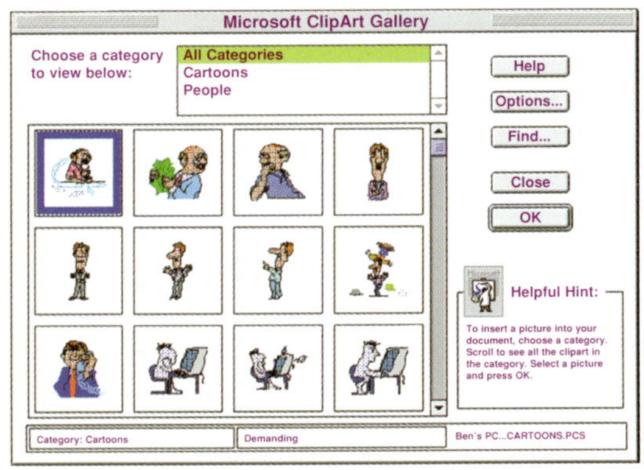

Clip Art dialog box

If you have a scanner, you can draw a picture by hand and scan it into your PC. You can use ready-made pictures. These are called Clip Art. They come with some word processing programs.

Liza also has a maths program on her computer. With it she can add and subtract, multiply and divide.

She also has lots of games programs. She often plays cards on her PC instead of doing her homework. What she likes most are games with monsters and mazes.

Networking

Ben longs to play games with Liza. "That's easy enough," says the Magic Mouse. "You can form a network."

Soon Liza and Ben's computers are linked up and Ben can share all Liza's games. Ben spends hours playing with them. The network includes a modem that links the computer to the internet. The internet is a vast network that covers the whole world.

On the internet you can:

- buy books and other items
- visit museums
- check the weather
- get the latest news
- look up information
- talk to people all round the world
- download free software and music

Ben looks up books and encyclopedias to help with his homework. He sends e-mails and faxes to his friends. He makes new friends on the internet.

His PC is the best present he has ever had.

More about computers

Active When you click on an icon or a window, it becomes active and opens up so that you can use it.

Backup Play safe and get your computer to keep a copy of your work. Then it will not be a disaster if you accidentally erase a document that you need.

CD See Compact disk.

CD-ROM A compact disk that you cannot erase. CD-ROMs can store large amounts of information, such as software programs and big encyclopedias.

Central processing unit The centre of the computer's brain, responsible for making the computer work and run programs.

Chip Short for microchip.

Clicking Pressing and quickly releasing the mouse button. To double click, quickly press and release the button twice. You will soon get to know when to click once and when to click twice.

Clip art Files of pictures in computer form that you can add to your documents to make them look good.

Compact disk Device that stores information electronically in a small amount of space.

Components The parts of a computer including the CPU, monitor and keyboard.

Computer pen An electronic pen that allows you to input work by drawing on the screen of the computer.

CPU See Central processing unit.

Cursor Arrow, line or other shape that appears on the screen to indicate where you are. You can move it about using the keyboard or the mouse.

Dialog box Pop-up box that lets you choose what you want to do next.

Digital camera A camera that you can plug into your computer to see the photographs you have taken on-screen.

Digital versatile disk Disc that can store very much more information than a CD-ROM.

Disk Round plate on which data is stored electronically. Disk can also be spelt disc.

Document Pages on which you can write or draw on-screen and print out.

DVD Short for digital versatile disk.

File A single document or computer program.

Floppy disk Small plastic disk coated with a magnetic layer on which you can store a small amount of information.

Folder A place in which to collect related documents, like a folder in a filing cabinet.

Fonts You can choose from many different looking typefaces, or fonts. You can change the size of the type or make it **bold** or *italic* or underline it.

Hard copy Anything that the computer prints out.

Hard disk drive Part of the computer where the programs and information that operate the computer itself are stored and where you can store programs and files.

Hardware The hard parts of a computer system including the computer itself.

Icon A picture of a file on the screen.

Internet A worldwide network of computers and information.

Joystick A lever that lets you move players in an electronic game

Keyboard The collection of keys that lets you enter words, numbers and commands.

Leads The wires that link the parts of a computer.

Maths program Software that does calculations for you.

Memory The computer's memory consists of a collection of microchips. Some store information that cannot be changed, others information that can be changed.

Menu A list of commands that gives you a choice of what to do next. Some choices open up dialog boxes.

Microchip A tiny chip of silicon on which electronic circuits are printed. These are the basic components of computers and other electronic gadgets from cars to washing machines.

Microprocessor A kind of microchip that carries out instructions from a software program.

Modem A device that links a computer to a telephone line and enables the user to send faxes and e-mails and gain access to the internet.

Monitor The screen attached to a computer. It is sometimes called a visual display unit, or VDU.

Mouse An electronic device attached to a computer. With it you can point, click, and drag. A mouse may have one button or more. When you click on an item you activate it. When you double-click you open it.

Music keyboard An electronic piano keyboard that enables you to compose or play music.

Network A group of computers connected by leads or telephone wires.

OK Option given in a dialog box. If you click on it, or press Enter or the Return key, the computer will carry out the set of commands you have chosen.

Operating system Program installed in your computer that works the computer itself and runs basic programs and allows it to communicate with you.

Paint program Software that allows you to draw and paint, and alter photographs.

Personal computer A computer designed for use in homes, schools and offices. More powerful computers are used in industry and in services like air-traffic control and traffic lights.

Power supply Electricity supplied from the mains or from a battery.

Program A list of instructions, written in computer language, for the computer to carry out.

RAM Stands for random access memory. RAM is used by the computer for storing information while a program is in use. You can change the program as much as you want. If you want to keep your work when the computer is switched off, you must save it. The computer will then store it on its hard disk.

ROM Stands for read only memory. This memory stores information permanently. Usually you cannot change it.

Scanner A device that lets you copy pictures or words into the computer.

Scroll To move through a document, up, down or across, by clicking the mouse, or using the arrow keys.

Shift Key that changes lower case (small) letters to CAPITALS. In combination with other keys, it also allows you to use additional keyboard characters.

Software A general name for computer programs.

Software program A set of instructions for the computer to carry out.

Spell checker A useful tool that checks spelling. It will pick up many errors but will not notice if you have missed a word or used the wrong word. Always check your work before you print it.

Toolbar A bar of buttons that appears at the top of the screen. Click on them to make the computer carry out tasks such as saving and printing.

Window A rectangular area on screen on which you can see and work on documents.

Word processor A software program that allows you to prepare letters, stories and anything written in type.

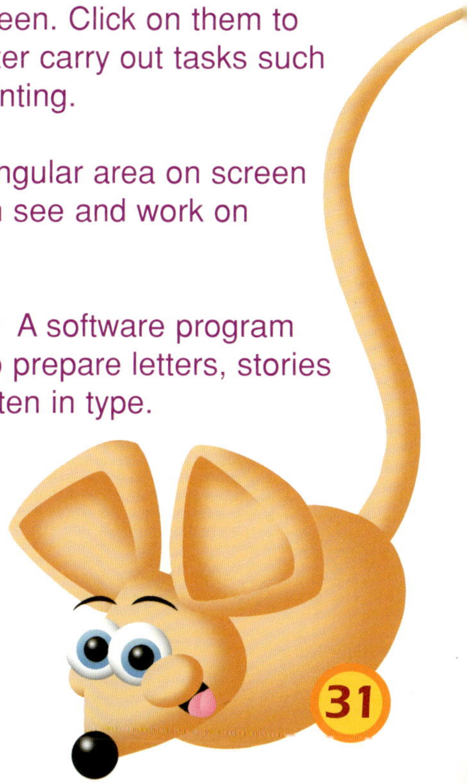

Index